Texas

Facts and Symbols

by Emily McAuliffe

Content Consultant:
Susie Kelly Flatau
Texas Folklore Society

Hilltop Books

An Imprint of Franklin Watts
A Division of Grolier Publishing
New York London Hong Kong Sydney
Danbury, Connecticut

Hilltop Books
http://publishing.grolier.com

Library of Congress Cataloging-in-Publication Data
McAuliffe, Emily.
    Texas facts and symbols/by Emily McAuliffe.
        p.   cm. -- (The states and their symbols)
    Includes bibliographical references (p. 23) and index.
    Summary: Presents information about the state of Texas, its nickname,
motto, and emblems.
    ISBN 1-56065-768-5
    1. Emblems, State--Texas--Juvenile literature. [1. Emblems, State--Texas.
2. Texas.] I. Title. II. Series: McAuliffe, Emily. States and their symbols.
CR203.T4M37 1998
976.4--dc21
                                                                        97-46009
                                                                             CIP
                                                                             AC

Editorial credits:
Editor, Rebecca Glaser; additional editing, Kim Covert; cover design, Clay
    Schotzko/Icon Productions; photo research, Michelle L. Norstad
Photo credits:
Dembinsky Photo Assoc., Inc./Stan Osolinski, 12; Adam Jones, 16
GEO Imagery/Jan W. Jorolan, cover
One Mile Up, Inc., 8, 10 (inset)
Cheryl R. Richter, 20
Six Flags Over Texas, 22 (middle)
Unicorn Stock Photos/Richard B. Dippold, 22 (top); Andre Jenny, 22 (bottom); Robert
    Vankirk, 10
Visuals Unlimited/Scott Berner, 6; Jeffrey Howe, 14; Tom Edwards, 18

Table of Contents

Fast Facts about Texas

Capital: Austin is the capital of Texas.

Largest City: Houston is the largest city in Texas. More than one million people live in Houston.

Size: Texas covers 268,601 square miles (698,363 square kilometers).

Location: Texas is in the southwestern United States. It is bordered by New Mexico, Oklahoma, Arkansas, Louisiana, and Mexico.

Population: 19,128,261 people live in Texas. (U.S. Census Bureau, 1996 estimate). Only California has more people than Texas.

Statehood: Texas became the 28th state on December 29, 1845.

Natural Resources: Companies in Texas mine oil, natural gas, and sulfur.

Manufactured Goods: Texans make goods from oil. They also make foods and machinery.

Crops: Farmers in Texas grow cotton, grains, and corn.

State Name and Nickname

Texas got its name from the Caddo word tejas (TAY-hawss). The Caddos were a group of Native American tribes. They lived in Texas. The Caddo people greeted friends by saying tejas.

People call Texas the Lone Star State. This nickname comes from the state flag. The flag has one white star. This is because Texas used to be a separate country. In 1845, Texas became part of the United States.

The Beef State is another nickname for Texas. Texans raise huge herds of cattle. The cattle live on large, open grasslands in the state. The Spanish brought cattle to Texas long ago. People named these cattle Texas longhorns.

People call Texas the Lone Star State. The Texas flag has one white star.

State Seal and Motto

The state seal is a small picture pressed into wax. Government officials stamp the picture onto important papers. The seal makes government papers official.

The state seal is a symbol. A symbol is an object that reminds people of something larger. For example, the U.S. flag reminds people of the United States.

The state seal of Texas shows one star. An oak branch and an olive branch circle the star. The oak branch stands for strength. The olive branch stands for peace.

Texas adopted this seal in 1839. Texas was not part of the United States at that time. It kept the same seal after it joined the United States.

The state motto is Friendship. A motto is a word or saying. Friendship has been the Texas state motto since 1930. Texans want everyone to know that friendly people live there.

Texas adopted its state seal in 1839.

State Capitol and Flag

Austin is the capital of Texas. A capital is the city where government is based.

The capitol building is also in Austin. Government officials work in the capitol. These officials make laws for the state.

Austin has the largest capitol in the country. Workers completed the capitol in 1888. They built it using stones from Texas.

Texans adopted the state flag in 1839. It has one white stripe and one red stripe. It also has a blue stripe. One white star sits in the middle of the blue stripe. This flag is called the Lone Star Flag.

Six national flags have flown over Texas. Spain, France, and Mexico each ruled Texas. Then Texas became independent. It flew the Republic of Texas flag. Texas flew the Confederate flag during the Civil War (1861-1865). It was part of the Confederate States of America during this time. Now Texas flies the flag of the United States.

Austin has the largest capitol in the country.

State Bird

The mockingbird is the state bird of Texas. It became the state bird in 1927. It is also the state bird of Arkansas, Florida, Mississippi, and Tennessee.

Adult mockingbirds are about 10 inches (25 centimeters) long. They have gray and white feathers and long tails.

Mockingbirds mock the songs of other birds. Mock means to copy. Mockingbirds can copy the songs of about 40 birds. They can also copy other sounds. They can even mock the sounds of barking dogs.

Mockingbirds build their nests from twigs. Their nests are cup-shaped. They make their nests in bushes or trees. Mockingbirds eat bugs, spiders, and fruits.

Female mockingbirds lay four to five eggs each year. The eggs are blue-green with brown spots. Mockingbirds are fearless when they guard their young. They will attack dogs, cats, and humans.

The state bird of Texas is the mockingbird.

State Tree

The pecan tree is the state tree of Texas. It became the state tree in 1919. Texas is the largest producer of pecan nuts. Pecan nuts grow on pecan trees. Texas was the first state to choose a state tree.

Pecan trees grow as tall as 180 feet (55 meters). Texans grow the trees mainly for pecan nuts. Companies use the wood from pecan trees to make furniture.

Pecan is a Native American word. It means nuts with hard shells. Many people like to eat pecan nuts. Cooks use the nuts to make cookies and pies.

James Hogg was the governor of Texas from 1891 to 1895. He was the first Texas governor who was born there. Hogg loved pecan trees. He even asked people to plant one beside his grave.

The pecan tree is the state tree of Texas.

State Flower

The state flower of Texas is the bluebonnet. The Texas government chose this flower in 1901. Some Texans call these flowers buffalo clovers or wolf flowers. Bluebonnets grow wild only in Texas. They must be planted in all other areas. Bluebonnets need lots of sun to grow. They bloom in the spring.

Bluebonnets have blue and white flowers. Each petal of the flower looks like a little bonnet. Petals are the colored outer parts of flowers. A bonnet is a hat tied with strings under the chin. Water drops rest in the bluebonnet's petals after a rainfall.

Different kinds of bluebonnets grow wild throughout Texas. The Big Bend bluebonnet grows in west Texas. It grows as tall as three feet (91 centimeters). The Texas bluebonnet grows in east Texas. It grows about 20 inches (51 centimeters) high.

Bluebonnets grow wild only in Texas.

State Mammals

Texas has three state mammals. A mammal is a warm-blooded animal with a backbone. Warm-blooded means that an animal's body heat stays the same. Its body heat does not change with the outside weather.

The big state mammal is the longhorn bull. The Texas government chose it in 1995. Longhorn bulls are a kind of cattle. Their horns are long and curved. Spanish people brought them to North America long ago. Texans raise huge herds of longhorn cattle.

The small state mammal of Texas is the armadillo. The Texas government chose it in 1995. Hard, bony plates cover the armadillo. The plates keep armadillos safe from enemies.

Texas also has a state flying mammal. It is the Mexican free-tailed bat. The Texas government chose it 1995. Mexican free-tailed bats eat insects. They live in caves and deserted tunnels in Texas.

Longhorn bulls have long, curved horns.

More State Symbols

State Dish: Chili became the state dish of Texas in 1977. Chili is a hot, spicy stew. People make chili with peppers, tomatoes, and beans.

State Fruit: The Texas red grapefruit became the state fruit in 1993. A grapefruit is a large, round fruit. It tastes both sweet and sour.

State Insect: The monarch butterfly became the state insect in 1995. An insect is a small animal with a hard outer shell. Insects have six legs. Some insects have wings. The monarch has orange wings with dark stripes and spots.

State Plant: The prickly pear cactus became the state plant in 1997. Cactuses grow sharp points instead of leaves. The prickly pear cactus produces a pear-shaped fruit.

State Sport: Rodeo became the state sport of Texas in 1997. People ride wild horses and bulls in rodeos.

Texans make chili with peppers.

Places to Visit

The Alamo

The Alamo is the most visited spot in Texas. The Alamo is an old church in downtown San Antonio. A small group of Texans fought at the Alamo in 1836. They were trying to keep Texas free. They fought Mexico's army. All of the Texans died as heroes.

Six Flags Over Texas

Six Flags Over Texas is an amusement park in Arlington. People go on rides and play games at amusement parks. Six Flags has more than 100 rides. One of them is the Texas Giant. Six Flags is named after the six flags that have flown over Texas.

Big Bend National Park

Big Bend National Park is in southwest Texas. The Rio Grande River forms the border between Mexico and Texas. The park got its name from the Rio Grande. The river makes a giant turn in the park. There are deserts, mountains, and deep valleys in the park.

Words to Know

amusement park (uh-MYOOZ-ment PARK)—a place where people go on rides and play games
capital (KAP-uh-tuhl)—the city where government is based
capitol (KAP-uh-tuhl)—the headquarters of state government
insect (IN-sekt)—a small animal with a hard outer shell and six legs; some insects have wings.
motto (MOT-oh)—a word or saying
rodeo (ROH-dee-oh)—a sporting event where people ride wild horses and bulls
state seal (STATE SEEL)—a small picture pressed into wax; the seal makes government papers official.
symbol (SIM-buhl)—an object that reminds people of something larger

Read More

Bredesen, Cannen. *Texas.* New York: Benchmark Books, 1994.

Capstone Press Geography Department. *Texas.* One Nation. Mankato, Minn.: Capstone Press, 1996.

Pelta, Kathy. *Texas.* Minneapolis: Lerner Publications Co., 1994.

Stein, R. Conrad. *Texas.* Chicago: Children's Press, 1994.

Useful Addresses

Texas Community Affairs
Travel and Information
Division
112 East 11th Street
Austin, TX 78701

Texas Department of State
Office of the Secretary of State
Capitol Building
Austin, TX 78701

Internet Sites

50 States and Capitals
http://www.scvol.com/States/main.htm
Lone Star Junction
http://www.lsjunction.com/
Texas Symbols
http://www.tpwd.state.tx.us/edu/texas/txsymbl.htm

Index